101
ENTREPRENEUR
MINDSET

How to have an Entrepreneur Mindset

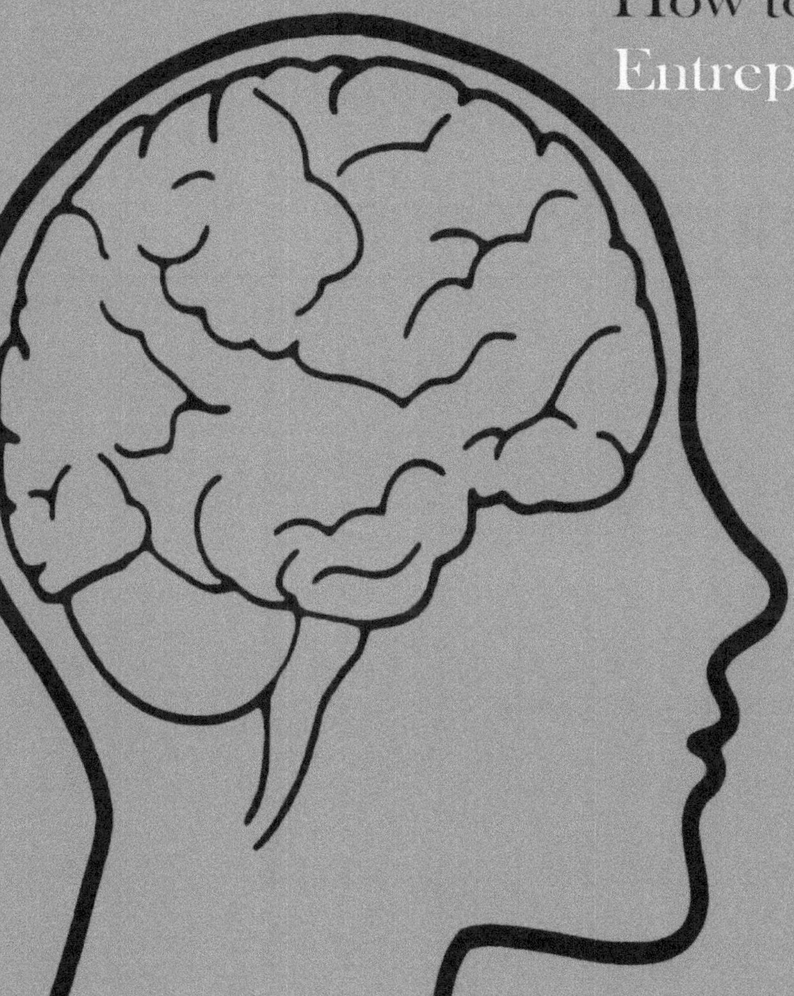

Vindimear D Heart

101 Entrepreneur Mindset

Vindimear D Heart

101 Entrepreneur Mindset

Copyright © 2015 by Vindimear D Heart

Table of Contents

Introduction   5
Chapter 1: Having an Entrepreneurial Mindset   6-9
Chapter 2: 7 Steps in Starting your Own Business   10-14
Chapter 3: Tips on Starting a Business   15-18
Chapter 4: 6 Things to Remember When Starting a Small Business   19-22
Chapter 5: A Beginner's Guide to Launching a Small Business   23-26
Chapter 6: Launching the Business   27-30
Conclusion   35
Author   36

Introduction

People who are employed nowadays are looking for a better source of income, especially if they are not happy working for a boss anymore. Most of these employees are seeking for opportunities to be the boss of their own. They want to have their own business and earn from it. If you are one of them, you must have an entrepreneur mindset.

You may have the talent and skills or a hardworking attitude, but are those things enough for you to survive a business for a long time? There are people who offer products and services, sell it online or to people in their network, but still having a hard time coping with the pressures of running their own business. They usually have no time for socialization, leisure, or even relaxation. They are also stuck in their current business standing, meaning they are not able to improve or innovate their business.

101 Entrepreneur Mindset

Chapter 1 : Having an Entrepreneurial Mindset

People who are employed nowadays are looking for a better source of income, especially if they are not happy working for a boss anymore. Most of these employees are seeking for opportunities to be the boss of their own. They want to have their own business and earn from it. If you are one of them, you must have an entrepreneur mindset.

You may have the talent and skills or a hardworking attitude, but are those things enough for you to survive a business for a long time? There are people who offer products and services, sell it online or to people in their network, but still having a hard time coping with the pressures of running their own business. They usually have no time for socialization, leisure, or even relaxation. They are also stuck in their current business standing, meaning they are not able to improve or to innovate their business.

An entrepreneur is an individual who operates, manages, and controls a business with the goal to earn profit. It is more than just having the talent and skills. Running a business needs to be properly and strategically planned; it also requires passion and discipline to build a business that will last and you will definitely enjoy doing. That is just some of the characteristics an entrepreneur must have. And to reach his goals, he must be:

1. Passionate

Passion is an important ingredient to achieve success in every business. This will take you to the highest of your potential to reach your goals.

Do your best and you will be able to exceed your limits as an entrepreneur. And to do your best, you must love what you are doing. If you want to be an entrepreneur, be the best entrepreneur that you can be. Having no passion for work will just make you lazy and procrastinate.

Even as you face problems in your business, passion will get you through it. As what Joseph Campbell, an American mythologist, writer, and lecturer said, "Passion will move men beyond themselves, beyond their shortcomings, beyond their failures."

2. Disciplined

In managing and organizing a business, one must have discipline in everything. The first and most important thing that you must manage is your time. A lot will suffer if you cannot manage time like making customers wait for delayed orders.

Avoid distractions that will take yourself away from finishing your work. You need to focus a lot more so that you can accomplish things in your business. If not, you will need to make more time to repair the damages or spend more time to finish your products or services.

There may also be changes from time to time about the demands of your customers and your capacity to work with them and their demands. These can stress you out and that is why you need to be flexible. Whatever changes that might happen in your business, you must be able to cope with them.

3. Optimistic

It is essential to have a mission and a vision for your business. This will help you forge a path toward your goals. Your mission and vision will always remind you what you want to happen in the future. But there will come a time that you will experience bumps in your business and will make you think twice if you can still achieve your mission and vision. Passion, of course, will help you but you also need optimism. It means having a positive response to a difficult situation.

Businesses can fail and go bankrupt but if you have an entrepreneur mindset, you will be optimistic that you will get through the challenges you are facing. Thus, you can think more positively and be more productive about looking for solutions than sulking and being sad about what happened. You would be able to think about new ideas, learn from your mistakes, and then build a new business venture.

4. A risk taker

As an entrepreneur, you must risk a lot of things especially money in creating your business. You must forget your fears and face the opportunities with confidence. From the start, you must know those risks that you will face in your chosen venture.

If you want to be more creative and innovative in your business, you must take risks to achieve better results and higher success.

5. A opportunity seeker

Being an entrepreneur means having the ability to find opportunities even in little things. Entrepreneurs see things that are normally not seen by ordinary people. They make the most out of everything they see as an opportunity. Even with the problems happening around them, they take them as opportunities — not only to build businesses but also to help solve problems related to their business. That's how broad the mind of an entrepreneur is.

6. A strategic planner

The main purpose of having a business is filling the needs of your chosen customers or your target market. You must know how to handle them in terms of their complaints. You must anticipate customer problems before they even happen. That is one way of strategic planning and strategic thinking. Before you actually encounter risks and problems, you know how to solve them because you have planned your strategies in the first place.

7. Persevering and persistent

Having a business is easy but managing and handling it is a different story. You have to face challenges, problems, risks, and shortcomings but those are normal. The secret is perseverance and persistence. Whatever challenges you may encounter throughout the course of your business, never give up.

Everyone has the talent and skills to start his or her own business but not everyone can be an entrepreneur. If you truly want to be an entrepreneur, then you must develop an entrepreneur mindset with the abovementioned traits and characteristics.

Chapter 2 : 7 Steps in Starting your Own Business

Working in a company seems like a bad idea for some people. They don't like working under a boss, having to be told what to do, and having the same routine every day because it can be boring for them. That's why these people have come up with the idea of building their own business.

There are three types of business: sole proprietorship, partnership, and corporation. You can choose from one of them depending on your resources at the moment.

Before starting a business, you must have the attitude of an entrepreneur. To have an entrepreneur mindset, you must be passionate, disciplined, optimistic, persevering, willing to take risks, able to seek opportunities, and know to plan strategically.

Here are **8** steps that you can follow to start your own business:

1. Think of a business idea.

Every person has that one idea that he wants to happen in his life. It is something that you would love to be part of your daily living because it makes you happy. It can be a talent or skill that you developed over the years. There are also ideas that just pop out of your mind while doing the dishes or when you are daydreaming. Just thinking about it makes you excited because you think it is your original idea — nobody has done it before! Or maybe, it is someone else's idea but you know you can do better. Everything and anything under the sun can be a business idea.

If you have that one idea that is superior from the others, ask for comments and suggestions from your friends or even people who are already experts in the business field. Learn from them, open up your creativity, and start planning your business idea.

2. Determine your purpose and goal.

To be a successful entrepreneur, you should know your purpose in establishing the business and the goals that you want to achieve.

In determining the purpose of your business, you must ask the question: "Why are you making this idea into a business?" Some would say they want to earn lots of money, help other people gain employment, or even because they want to change the world. Every entrepreneur must have his own purpose. If not, the business will not last. The entrepreneur will not have the drive to continue what he had started. That is why having a purpose is very important.

Business goals are what lead you to the right path and direction. All businesses must have vision. What do you want to achieve and reach in the future? Do you want an innovation of your products and services? Do you want to expand and build even more branches? Everything is possible as long as you know where you are going and how to get there.

And always remember, the main purpose of your business is to satisfy your customers, attend to their needs, and solve customer problems.

3. Decide on a business name.

This is a critical decision to make. It will greatly affect the success of the business. The wrong choice of name can cost you your customers and your profitability. But the right choice of name can even make your business the most famous one in town.

A business name must be something that relates to your product or service. It should not be confusing or too long. Make it short and simple so customers will remember it well. Make it unique so you can be different from other businesses. Be creative and take lots of time to think about it.

4. Write a business plan.

This is the most important part in starting your business. This is where you plan everything that is needed to launch the business. There is a business plan format that you can follow, though it can be different depending on the type of business that you are going to build.

A business plan includes a brief description of a project. It describes the type of business, business idea, name and logo, products or services, objectives, and location.

There are four aspects that a business plan needs to discuss: the marketing aspect, the organizational aspect, the technical aspect, and the financial aspect. The marketing aspect discusses your target market and how will you advertise your service and product to them. The organizational aspect discusses the team that will help you in the business and their job descriptions. The technical aspect discusses the description of the products and services you will offer. And lastly, the financial aspect discusses the business' potential to gain or lose profit.

5. Know the resources you need and get them.

Now that you have your business plan, you must gather the resources that you need, such as things in making your products or the machines, tools, and equipment for the services you will offer. Your resources may also include the people to work for you.

6. Advertise your products and services.

You have a lot of choices on how you are going to market your products and services. The first one is through word-of-mouth. Make sure to let your family, friends, classmates, co-workers, and acquaintances know about your business. That will pave a way for their contacts to know about it, too.

The second method is through written materials. Advertising through newspapers, magazines, brochures, and flyers is an old way but that can help as well.

The third and last method is through the Web. Almost everyone nowadays uses the Internet to surf and/or socialize. You can make use of Facebook, Twitter, Instagram, and other social networking sites to make your products and services known.

Be flexible — if one method does not work, you can always try the other two.

7. Launch your business.

You can finally open your business, May it be online or an actual store. It's the last step in starting your business. But, it is the first step in making your business idea become successful. The first six steps will help you get started and settled in your first business operations. This last step will make your business idea a reality, and it is up to you to follow it through.

Chapter 3: Tips on Starting a Business

From every part of the world, there are new businesses cropping up, offering new products and services that were not even available before. Anyone can start a business as long as they have the resources but not everyone can be an entrepreneur.

Being an entrepreneur is not an easy job. Starting your own business requires a lot of effort. It will give you problems, stress, challenges, and risks. It's normal for a business to face those things. It will all be worth it as long as you can overcome those obstacles. An entrepreneur knows what it takes to succeed and these tips will help you have the entrepreneur mindset needed in starting a business.

There are 5 mindsets that you should to have before starting a business

1. Have the right business attitude.

Talent and skill will take you places but having the right approach will determine your success. Other entrepreneurs may have studied business management for years or attended lots of business seminars — but those still cannot be enough. There are certain characteristics and traits that you need to be an effective and successful entrepreneur.

Being disciplined, passionate, innovative, self-confident, honest, optimistic, flexible, and hardworking are some of the traits that make up an entrepreneur mindset. You can learn and develop these traits, except for passion. You can only find passion within yourself. Always keep it alive.

2. Enhance your creativity.

You will be surprised how far your mind can travel to. Everyone has the capability to be innovative and unique. From your childhood up to the present, you have developed a certain level of creativity. And you can excel in a certain skill or talent that you have accumulated through the years. For example, a photographer knows how to analyze visual arts, while a pianist is able to analyze the relationship of the notes.

In business, you can be innovative in producing new products or services that were not available in the market before. Here are some ways to fine-tune your business creativity:

- Research what has been done and what has not been done yet. Or you may also develop an idea that is available already.

- Acquire learnings and experiences by attending classes or seminars, be they local or international.

- Meet new people and share ideas. It may be the start of a fruitful partnership. You can also meet people who have opposite or different views and ideas from you. You may learn from them.

- Gather your team and brainstorm for more ideas. Asking the suggestions of your team will also help them realize their value and contribution to the business.

- Be informed about the needs of the society. You might come up with an idea that will help people from all over the world.

These are just some helpful tips to reach the level of creativity that you want to have the best business ideas. Always seek for resources available to train and develop your creativity.

3. Always be on the lookout for new business innovations.

Being creative and innovative is closely related to each other. A new innovation in your business is the result of your creativity in making business ideas.

Innovation is important for a growing business. Without it, the business will be stuck and will not be able to go forward.

People have a never-ending need for satisfaction. They always ask for more. They are never contented. That is why businesses need to improve their products and services to the next level. A restaurant having the same menu for 30 years won't be successful for a long time. You can maintain certain dishes but you must add or improve the others. This will make your customers curious. They will keep on trying the new things you offer them. Thus, you will be able to keep your customers happy and expand your reach for as long you innovate.

4. Be adaptable to changes

Change is the only constant thing in this world. You may be on top of your business right now but what about tomorrow? It is always uncertain. Your first few years in handling the business might be smooth but the next few years might bring lots of challenges and problems that may push you to take equally lots of risks. With the changes in your business, the trait that you must have in order to survive and flourish is flexibility.

One aspect of business that needs your flexibility is the pricing. The economic stability of a country is not always guaranteed. There will come a time that you need to adjust your prices so you can maintain your business' profitability. Your customers will surely react to these price hikes but you must have your plans ahead to solve this issue. You can do packages or add-ons so that they will not complain so much about the price hike you just did with your products and/or services.

It's just one example of a problem you may face in the future. Always be ready for them and plan ahead. Remember that every now and then, changes will occur and your business should learn how to cope with them.

5. Be savvy when it comes to solving customer problems.

Customers are what keep the business alive. They are one of the main reasons that one started the business in the first place. That is why one always needs to know and anticipate their needs and give them satisfaction.

There will always be complaints and negative feedback but learn to attend to them in a nice way. Address your customers' complaints and problems so you can guarantee repeat guests and maintain a good business reputation.

These are just a few tips but following these will help you in your business' challenges in the future. Remember these to help you reach your goals and success.

Chapter 4 : 6 Things to Remember When Starting a Small Business

Starting a small business is a dream of many people who are seeking financial independence. While operating a business may seem difficult and overwhelming, you can actually make it enjoyable, exciting, and incredibly satisfying by preparing yourself physically, mentally, and emotionally for the tasks ahead. All the hard work will definitely be worth it after you feel the sense of fulfillment and pleasure that the actual launching of your business will bring.

The preparation and planning period need not be too long or complex as the best way to launch a business is to simply do it. You will soon find out that no amount of preparation can make you ready for all the issues that you will potentially face once your enterprise starts running. But you will never start and accomplish anything unless you start, right?

This short guide will help you get yourself ready on how to effectively manage a startup venture from the ground up. Reading this article is important in order to have a strong and stable foundation in handling a startup business. But keep in mind that you should always be open for continuous learning as you gain more experience in your endeavor.

If you have really decided to become a full-pledged entrepreneur, here are six things to remember:

1. Set the right attitude

The best way to launch a new business is to just launch it. However, if you don't have the right mindset and the proper perspective, you can complicate the process for yourself.

Ask yourself some important questions like: Am I ready to spend most of my time on this endeavor? What are the things I'm willing to give up to make this thing work? Am I ready to serve other people and put their needs first before mine? These are just some of the questions that you should contemplate on because in reality, the main reason successful businesses exist is they serve people and solve their particular problems efficiently.

Also, create a clear and concrete vision and always think of the big picture so that you will not lose track of your goals. You can break down your goals into separate, short-term objectives and focus on them one at a time to make the vision more attainable. As you one by one finish your short-term objectives, you will keep yourself motivated to move on to the next steps until the whole thing is accomplished.

2. Keep creative enthusiasm

Do sufficient research before actually starting up. Read all the literature that you can about your particular business niche. Know what your competitors and the top companies are doing. Try to learn more about their best practices and get your artistic juices flowing by integrating them and making them applicable to your own plans and situation.

Don't completely copy what others have done and are doing as the best businesses offer their own original specialty to prospective clients and customers.

Make your brand stand out by crafting your very own USP (Unique Selling Proposition). Your USP is the thing that you will be known for and make sure that you are ready to deliver it to all your forthcoming customers 100% of the time.

3. Start simple

You don't need to keep up with the latest technical innovation at once when you are just beginning. Don't think about the most expensive grinding machine, for example, and just kick off with what you can acquire that is within your startup capital. Time will come when you will be able to afford all the improvements you want to make, but that time won't come unless you begin right now.

You don't need the best equipment as of the moment. What you need is the right equipment to perform and deliver your products and services to the best of your abilities.

4. Always be flexible

Adaptability is crucial if you want your startup to be successful. You must always remember and accept wholeheartedly that not everything will take place perfectly according to what you have planned. If you refuse to believe this, then you are setting yourself up for a lot of frustrations, disappointments, and even discouragements.

This goes on to say that you should also make simple but helpful contingency plans. For instance, instead of having just one supplier of raw materials to connect with, have at least three so that you will not be drained of inventory when the time comes.

5. You don't have to do everything by yourself

Another important reminder when just starting out is that you don't have to place all the burden on yourself. If you are not an accountant, then you can always hire a professional to do the stuff for you. You just need to oversee everything and make sure that all the important details are being worked out. You may just misuse your starting capital if you do something wrong that has to be revised later; so better just let someone do it right the first time.

6. Quality customer service

Finally, a good startup must be able to solve customer problems well to begin attracting new patrons. There is nothing more powerful than word-of-mouth marketing and it can be quickly achieved by always giving the best value to your customers. If you are able to excel in this aspect of your business, then you can be sure that you have at least one foot inside the success door already.

If possible, set up a 24-hour customer support system online where your customers can contact you in at least three different mediums: by phone, by email, and through a website. For a more effective approach, you can also establish your company's own social media accounts. However, when you do this, make sure that all your online accounts are well managed. Once you expose your business this way, customers will expect to receive responses as soon as possible. While it may seem difficult, the rewards of customer loyalty will mean a lot eventually.

Chapter 5 : A Beginner's Guide to Launching a Small Business

You may have been inspired by the accomplishments of the wealthy and powerful business people that you have read about in magazines and newspapers. All of them are financially independent, and you may have wanted to follow their footsteps but didn't know how and where to start. The good news is that none of them is an overnight success and all have worked their way up to where they are now.

Launching a business, even a small one, can be a pretty intimidating task, especially for a budding entrepreneur. The steps below will guide you on how to do it - and do it right the first time.

Six Steps When Launching Your Business

1. Prepare yourself

It's ironic, but the journey to actually launching a new business begins within you. You must first examine yourself before even doing anything. And then get yourself ready once you have really decided to pursue your dream venture. It's all about your attitude and your emotional stability when it comes to opening a startup enterprise. Inspiration and motivation are crucial when preparing you to kick off a new business.

List down all of the things that you are passionate about; things that you would do even when you don't get paid such as cooking, writing, or playing a musical instrument. You can begin with these when thinking about what type of business would suit you best. Afterward, evaluate your daily schedule.

Which activities are you willing to give up to make time for successfully launching and running a startup? Also, research and read a lot to learn more about the venture that you are going to pursue, even the risks and common issues. It would save you loads of trouble if you are aware of these things from the beginning.

2. Craft a business plan

A business plan is highly important for a startup, especially if you intend to ask financial support from potential investors or if you are going to make a loan to fund your venture. Almost all banks and financial institutions require an officially crafted business plan to lend money to a borrowing business owner. And even though you do not mean to borrow money from anyone, a well-written business plan will give you focus, guidance, and motivation to continue moving on when things get tough.

Be creative when writing your business plan. A standard business plan includes all your long-term goals, short-term goals, and all your specific strategies and action plans to achieve them. These goals include a lot of aspects such as financing, production, quality control, customer service, branding, and marketing.

3. Raise your capital

As mentioned above, your well-crafted business plan will help you a lot when seeking sufficient capital for your startup. Seeking funds for your venture should not be too difficult. Just always keep in mind that you don't need a very huge amount of money when just starting. You only need an initial investment that you can cultivate and grow.

There are actually many ways to fund your business, such as asking for donations, looking for investors, getting a partner, applying for a loan, or have it crowdfunded. All it takes is a little innovation and ingenuity to figure out which are the best ways that you can build your capital.

4. Decide on a structure

Make up your mind whether you are going to dive in as a sole proprietor, in a partnership, or as a corporation. Choosing the right business structure will greatly affect how you would manage your startup, from naming your enterprise to filing your taxes. Each business structure has its own advantages and disadvantages so you better research each one to know what type do you prefer the most.

However, if you are a novice entrepreneur, it is highly recommended to start out as a sole proprietor for your company to become more flexible and to make things simpler and decision-making faster. Besides, you can always modify your business structure anytime you want in the future whenever you feel that there is a need to change.

5. Register your business

The next step after you have crafted your business plan, raised your capital, and decided on a structure is to finally register your business. The name of your startup is more important than what you may think. Although you can also change it anytime (and it comes with some fees), you would not want to plunge in on the wrong foot. You can find many articles in the web on how to effectively name a business, so you can easily research on this.

After deciding on a business name, you will then have to check whether the name is already in use or not. If it is original then there would be no problems registering it. Then you can now move on to acquiring permits, licenses, and all the other legal documents of your startup.

6. Set up an accounting system

Probably one of the best advice that a newbie entrepreneur could receive before the actual launch of his business is to set up an accounting system first. Without a properly running accounting system, you will have problems the moment you serve your first customer onwards. With appropriate accounting, you can also solve customer problem from billings and invoices as soon as possible.

While it is so essential, you don't have to buy high-end accounting software right away. You can start with basic spreadsheets or you can hire an accountant to be sure.

Chapter 6 : Launching the Business

After completing the six steps above, the only thing left to do is to essentially launch your dream business. Don't forget to execute a well-planned marketing strategy a month or two before your actual business launch to ensure that everything will be a success.

Do You Want to Start Your Own Business?

A lot of people have also thought about becoming a full-pledged entrepreneur and launching their own businesses the same as you. And almost all of them are held back by the same feeling of confusion and pressure that the work of starting one seems to imply.

While starting a business is really not an easy task and not for the faint of heart, it is not that complicated and overwhelming as well. Anybody can start a company and be successful. As long as you have the proper guidance, attitude, knowledge, foresight, motivation, and a clear vision of what you want to attain, then anything is possible for you.

If you are one of the many who want to join the ranks of being a thriving entrepreneur, read on as here are a few essential tips on how to successfully start your own business:

1. Think of a common problem

Successful companies are those that solve common real life problems. If your business idea does not solve any specific human difficulty or crisis, then it will most likely fail in the long run.

There are many ways on how to come up with a common problem to solve. One is to conduct a market research on the things that make people feel upset and uncomfortable. A good example of this is the group that created the selfie stick.

Another way of doing it, and perhaps the easiest, is to actually observe yourself and notice the things that you are inconvenient about. For instance, the inventor of the coffee cup cardboard sleeve, Jay Sorensen, was inspired by his own problem of being burned by a hot cup of coffee over and over again. And the rest, so to speak, is history.

2. Be original

Be unique and creative. Don't carbon copy what anyone else has done and strive to offer the real you. This is not to say that you ignore what everyone else is doing. In fact, it is good to know the products and the best practices of your potential business rivals and those that are the best in your niche. You may take a little from everyone and create your own version of a product or service.

The important thing here is that people will know you for what you can specifically provide for them. For example, there are a lot of companies right now that are manufacturing customized caps, shirts, pens, and other paraphernalia. Be unique by offering them direct, hands on involvement from the design and conceptualization process, to the finalization, and up to mass production. It is as if making the customer feel that he owns your company.

3. Prepare the best product or service

Make sure that the product or service you will be offering to your prospective clients is something that you yourself will also use and buy. That should be the measure of how good your business can be. You can also try creating a sample object or process first and let a small group of testers experience them and give you honest feedback. Do it until you get a satisfying response.

However, upgrading does not stop the moment you launch your product or business. You should never stop reaching for perfection, and your products and services should be continuously evolving. Innovation is important for a thriving business, and it is directed by constant improvement.

4. Write a business plan

Writing a proper business plan is essential if you want to solicit capital from friends and family members, and most especially from prospective veteran investors. Most banks and financial institutions who offer loans also require a duly notarized business plan before approval.

Not only will it help you raise funds, a well-crafted strategy and proposal can also give you clarity and direction when it comes to achieving all your targets and objectives. A great business plan is specific, doable, and flexible. Aside from the main vision and goals, it should also contain smaller specific goals and action plans.

5. Engage with customers

Specifically target the demographic that you want to serve with your pre-launch marketing efforts. Yes, you read it right. Marketing can take place even before a business starts. In fact, it is important to do a lot of marketing work prior to the actual launch of your venture. Interacting with potential customers can be highly beneficial once your product or service is out there in the market. Spreading awareness that you can solve customer problem reliably and efficiently is best done before, and not after, a business launch.

As already mentioned in the previous items, one way to do this is to select a small group of customers first and let them try out your product or service. They can be your friends, relatives, or acquaintances. Ask them not only for honest comments, but also to help you promote your business once it launches.

Another medium for successful pre-launch marketing is through blogs and social media. Connect with an influential blogger and let him or her write about what you have to offer. Create your company's own social media accounts and share there what your business is all about.

6. Don't quit your job yet

Lastly, don't quit your job before launching your own business. Allow a few months for your startup to become stable before resigning. A lot of new entrepreneurs have failed because of the mistake of quitting their jobs too soon. Remember that you still need a steady income stream to sustain your everyday needs, and your new business may not be able to give it to you initially. As a matter of fact, your startup may need more cash outputs during the beginning stages to be used for licensing, advertising, and other legal and mandatory stuff.

Conclusion

All the topic of this book will guide you and help you to get an idea to think about new business and how to launch a startup business with creative way and also using a right mindset to set the direction to get your goal in the future.

And thank you for purchasing my book and I hope this book will help you more or less. Please take a look our book with new topic and new knowledge for you to collect.

Author

My name is Theeradech Thapanaphong and I have experience in many fields as Medical field, Astrology Field, Career Field, Outsource, and Consultant. I shared all my skill and experience to this book and we want to give my knowledge to all the audiences.